Mrs. C[illegible] in Alligator Alley

Written by Jill Eggleton
Illustrated by Philip Webb

Rigby

Mrs. O'Malley loved to dilly-dally in Alligator Alley.

One day she got a letter.
It said . . .

Mrs. O'Malley was angry.
She went to see the mayor
and she said . . .

"I want to dilly-dally
in Alligator Alley.
I want to dilly-dally, I do!
If alligators snap their
jaws at me,
I will just say . . .
shoo, shoo, shoo!"

MAYOR
MAYOR

But the mayor said,
"Don't be silly,
Mrs. O'Malley.
Alligators are fierce!"

MAYOR
MAYOR

Mrs. O'Malley was angry,
so she went downtown
and she said to the people
in the street . . .

"I want to dilly-dally
in Alligator Alley.
I want to dilly-dally, I do!
If alligators snap their
jaws at me,
I will just say . . .
shoo, shoo, shoo!"

Bookshop
MOLLY'S
Café
FOOD

But the people
in the street said,
"Don't be silly,
Mrs. O'Malley.
Alligators are ferocious!"

Mrs. O'Malley was angry.
She went home to think.
"I could tie up
the alligators' jaws.
But alligators are fierce."

"I could take the alligators somewhere else.
But alligators are ferocious."

"I know, I could make a net for Alligator Alley."

So Mrs. O'Malley
made a net.
It was huge.
It was **humongous**.
It was like a giant web.
And the alligators loved it.

DANGE

Mrs. O'Malley said to the alligators...

"I want to dilly-dally
in Alligator Alley.
I want to dilly-dally,
you see.
And you can snap
and snap your jaws,
But you won't, won't,
won't snap me."

Mrs. O'Malley went to sleep
on the grass.
But when she woke up,
there were people
everywhere!
And they were shouting . . .

"Look at that net.
It is huge.
It is **humongous**.
It is like a giant web.
Now we can dilly-dally
in Alligator Alley!"

But Mrs. O'Malley said. . .

"No, you can't!
I want to dilly-dally
in Alligator Alley.
I want to dilly-dally, I do.
I want to dilly-dally
in Alligator Alley.
So **shoo, shoo, shoo!**"

"**Wow**," said the people.
And they ran away
shouting . . .

"Mrs. O'Malley is fierce.
Mrs. O'Malley is ferocious.
We can't dilly-dally
in Alligator Alley!

Not with Mrs. O'Malley!"

Guide Notes

Title: Mrs. O'Malley in Alligator Alley
Stage: Early

Genre: Fiction
Approach: Shared Reading
Processes: Thinking Critically, Exploring Language, Processing Information
Written and Visual Focus: Signs, Letters, Insignia

THINKING CRITICALLY

(sample questions)

- What do you think this story could be about?
- How do you think Mrs. O'Malley felt about getting a letter from the mayor?
- How do you know it is an important letter?
- What else do you think Mrs. O'Malley could do with the alligators?
- Why do you think the alligators liked the net Mrs. O'Malley made?
- Why do you think Mrs. O'Malley didn't want any people in Alligator Alley?
- Do you think this story could be true? Why/Why not?

EXPLORING LANGUAGE

Terminology

Title, cover, illustrations, author, illustrator

Vocabulary

Interest words: humongous, dilly-dally, ferocious, fierce, jaws
Compound words: everywhere, somewhere, downtown
Contractions: can't, won't

Print Conventions

Capital letter for sentence beginnings and names (**M**rs. **O'M**alley, **A**lligator **A**lley), periods, exclamation marks, quotation marks, commas, ellipses